To all you seekers—

The dreamers, the believers, the ones who dare to ask for more.

This book is for you. For those who know there is something greater beyond the seen, who trust in the unseen forces guiding their path, and who are ready to step into their power as conscious creators of their destiny.
May this journey ignite your spirit, awaken your potential, and remind you that the universe is always conspiring in your favor.

With love and light

21 Days of Manifestation

A step by step guide to manifesting your dream life

NUTAN KHURANA
MANISHA ABBASI

Nutan Khurana and Manisha Abbasi
1st Edition

Publication Date : February 2025
Price : Rs. 295 , $ 6.99
ISBN : 978-93-49571-62-4
Published by: The Great Indian Book Tour
Imprint: Holistic Publishing
Website : https://essence2expression.co.in/
E-mail : essence2expression@gmail.com

Table of Contents

Acknowledgement

Writing this book has been a journey of growth, reflection, and transformation, and we could not have done it alone.

To our families— the foundation of our journey. Your encouragement has given us the strength to follow our purpose, and for that, we are forever grateful.

To our friends— Your presence in our lives has been a constant reminder of the power of connection and shared energy.

To Daraab- A very special thanks to Daraab for his keen creative eye and all the beautiful artwork. His dedication and artistic brilliance have been invaluable, and we are deeply appreciative of his contributions.

To every soul who has crossed our path—whether you brought joy, lessons, challenges, or encouragement—thank you. Each experience has contributed to our growth and has given us a deeper understanding of the power we all hold to create our reality.

And finally, to you, our reader—thank you for embarking on this journey of manifestation and self-discovery. Your willingness to open your heart and mind to new possibilities is a gift, and we are honored to be a part of your transformation.

May this book serve as a guiding light as you step into your power and manifest the life you truly desire.

Love...Light...Power to all!!

Dear Readers........

First and foremost, we want to express our deepest gratitude for your unwavering support of our previous book, ReCreate Your Destiny. Your dedication to transforming your life and embracing the power within you was nothing short of inspiring.. The feedback we received from so many of you was truly heartwarming, and we are thrilled to continue this journey together.

As you hold this new book, 21 Days of Manifestation, in your hands, know that it is a natural extension of everything we began with ReCreate Your Destiny. Many of you have reached out to share how ReCreate Your Destiny shifted your perspectives, helped you break through old patterns, and opened the doors to new possibilities. But some of you shared your concern and need for something more hands-down approach, a clear and concise method to achieve the goals. So here we are, with a more comprehensive step-by-step guide, to manifest your goals faster Now, with 21 Days of Manifestation, we're taking all of that momentum and building upon it. We're diving even deeper into the process of co-creating with the universe, manifesting your dreams, and aligning your actions with your highest vision.

While ReCreate Your Destiny was about awakening your true power, 21 Days of Manifestation is about putting that power to work in practical, intentional ways. This book offers a daily framework that will guide you through exercises, reflections, and practices that will reprogram your subconscious mind, clarify your desires, and help you take inspired action toward your goals. By the end of this 21-day journey, we believe you'll look back and realize just how much transformation you've experienced—not only in your external reality but also within yourself.

You've already shown that you're committed to changing your life, and we are so excited to be with you every step of the way as you manifest your dreams and create the future you've always wanted. Together, we will make magic happen. You've already taken the first step, and we can't wait to see where this new journey takes you.

Thank you for trusting us once again. We are beyond excited to witness the transformations that will unfold as you work through 21 Days of Manifestation and continue to create your destiny.
With heartfelt gratitude and excitement for what lies ahead,

Nutan & Manisha

Introduction
21 Days of Manifestation

"21 Days of Manifestation" is designed as a sacred journey of self-discovery, empowerment, and manifestation. This book isn't just about achieving goals; it's about shifting your mindset, embodying your true potential, and learning how to consciously co-create with the universe. It's about becoming the person who can not only envision the life you desire but also take the inspired actions necessary to manifest it.

Throughout the next three weeks, you'll encounter a series of daily practices that will deepen your understanding of manifestation and guide you toward creating the life you desire. These exercises aren't meant to be rushed through; rather, they are designed to help you pause, reflect, and take inspired action. Each day builds upon the previous one, creating a powerful momentum that will help you manifest your dreams in a way that feels authentic, aligned, and deeply fulfilling.

While 21 days may seem like a small amount of time, it is more than enough to set powerful intentions, break free from self-doubt, and tap into the energy of the universe. The process outlined in this book is designed to help you take consistent, intentional steps each day, gradually shifting your reality from one of limitation to one of limitless possibility.

The 21-day framework is not arbitrary. It is based on the principle that it takes 21 days to establish a new habit or mindset. By committing to these practices every day, you will begin to shift your subconscious programming and unlock new levels of possibility.As you embark on this journey, remember that manifestation is a personal experience. What works for one person may not work for another, and that's perfectly okay. This book offers a variety of tools, practices, and techniques—feel free to tailor them to suit your own needs, desires, and lifestyle. Trust yourself, trust the process, and remain open to the infinite possibilities that await you.

Manifestation is not just about achieving tangible outcomes—it's also about creating a mindset and lifestyle that supports your greatest good. It's about moving through life with a sense of purpose, joy, and alignment. By the end of these 21 days, you will begin to see how powerful you truly are. You will gain clarity, focus, and direction. You will uncover the limiting beliefs that have held you back and replace them with empowering thoughts that align with your dreams. You will take inspired actions that lead to real-world changes. And most importantly, you will start to experience the joy and fulfillment that comes with consciously creating the life you desire.

The journey to manifestation starts now. You are about to embark on a path of transformation, self-discovery, and empowerment that will change the way you experience life.

Welcome to 21 Days of Manifestation.

Let's begin

The Power of Manifestation

Manifestation is more than a concept; it's a universal law and an ancient truth woven into the fabric of humanity's collective wisdom. From the rituals of ancient civilizations to modern-day affirmations and visualization practices, the essence of manifestation has transcended time and culture. It's the art of creating reality by channeling your thoughts, emotions, and actions toward a specific outcome. Personally, I have come to see it not as a mystical idea but as a deeply transformative force—a tool that can shift not only what happens around you but who you become in the process.

When I first encountered the concept of manifestation, it sounded almost too good to be true. Could my thoughts and feelings really shape my reality? I was skeptical. But over time, as I experimented with this practice and saw undeniable shifts in my own life, I realized manifestation is not a magic trick or wishful thinking. Instead, it's a deliberate process that begins within and radiates outward, blending inner belief with inspired action.

At its core, manifestation is the process of turning your desires into reality by aligning your inner world—your thoughts, beliefs, and emotions—with the outer world of experiences and circumstances. It's about creating harmony between what you deeply wish for and the energy you project into the universe.

I have learned that manifestation is not about controlling every detail of life or expecting instant results. Instead, it's about embracing your role as a co-creator with the universe. For example, I remember when I first wanted to transition into a more fulfilling career. At the time, I wasn't sure how it could happen, but I began to focus on what that future would feel like. I visualized myself thriving, doing meaningful work, and connecting with like-minded individuals. This clarity became a magnet, drawing opportunities and people into my life that made the dream a reality.

Manifestation applies to all areas of life—your health, relationships, finances, personal growth, and beyond. What I find fascinating is how interconnected these areas can be. When you work on manifesting better health, for instance, you might find your relationships also improving as you bring more positivity and balance into your life.

How Does It Work?

The power of manifestation lies in your ability to focus and direct energy. The universe operates on vibrational frequencies, and the energy you emit—shaped by your thoughts, emotions, and beliefs—determines the frequency you're aligned with. In simpler terms, you attract what you are. If you emit joy, gratitude, and confidence, you're more likely to draw experiences that resonate with those emotions.

This alignment doesn't happen overnight. For me, it required shifting old patterns of doubt and fear. I began by identifying limiting beliefs that had held me back—beliefs like "I'm not good enough" or "success is out of reach." Replacing those with empowering ones like "I am worthy of success" and "abundance flows freely to me" was a game-changer.

I've found that one of the most overlooked aspects of manifestation is action. Manifestation isn't passive; it requires you to meet the universe halfway. For instance, if you want financial abundance, it's not just about visualizing wealth but also taking practical steps, such as budgeting, learning new skills, or seeking out opportunities. Action amplifies your intention, proving to yourself and letting the universe know that you are serious about what you want.

The Law of Attraction

One of the most transformative principles, a cornerstone of manifestation is the **Law of Attraction**. This universal law states that like attracts like your energy, thoughts, and emotions are magnets that draw corresponding experiences into your life. At first, this idea seemed almost magical to me, but as I observed my life and intentionally applied this law, I realized how deeply practical and profound it is.

When you radiate positivity, gratitude, and belief in your dreams, the universe responds in kind, presenting opportunities, people, and circumstances that align with your vibration. But the Law of Attraction isn't simply about thinking happy thoughts and expecting miracles; it's about embodying the energy of your desires and acting as though they are already a part of your life.

The Law of Attraction is not just a principle—it's a lifestyle. By aligning your thoughts, emotions, and actions with your desires, you become a powerful co-creator of your reality. Remember, manifestation is not about forcing outcomes; it's about cultivating the energy of what you want and trusting the universe to meet you where you are.

As you move forward, embrace the process with faith, patience, and inspired action. Celebrate small victories along the way, and know that the universe is always conspiring in your favor. The life you dream of is not only possible—it's waiting for you to claim it.

How This Book Works

Welcome to 21 Days of Manifestation. Over the next three weeks, you will embark on a transformative journey that will deepen your understanding of the manifestation process. Still, before you dive in, it's important to understand how this book is designed to support you in your manifestation journey and how you can get the most out of it.

Manifestation is not a one-size-fits-all approach. Each person's journey is unique, and the way you connect with your desires and intentions will be as individual as you are. This book offers a structure that allows you to customize your practice while following a clear and effective path. In this chapter, I will explain how the next 21 days are organized and how to best approach each day's exercises.

The 21-Day Framework

The 21-day structure is based on the idea that it takes about 21 days to create a new habit or shift your mindset. During this time, your intention is to build a consistent, daily practice that allows you to focus on what you want to manifest while rewiring old patterns and beliefs. By the end of this journey, you will not only have stronger manifestation abilities but also a deeper understanding of yourself, your desires, and the power you have to shape your reality.

Each day will focus on a different aspect of the manifestation process. These daily lessons are designed to help you build momentum and gradually shift your energy towards the reality you wish to create. Whether it's clarifying your goals, clearing limiting beliefs, or taking inspired action, each day's exercise is intended to deepen your connection with your desires and the universe.

How Each Day is Structured

To make your experience as effective as possible, each day in 21 Days of Manifestation follows a simple and consistent structure. Here's a breakdown of what you can expect each day:

1. Introduction to the Theme of the Day

Each day begins with a short introduction that outlines the key theme or topic you will focus on. This could range from setting clear intentions to releasing resistance or taking inspired action. The introduction sets the tone for the day and prepares you to engage with the exercises that follow.

2. Daily Manifestation Exercise

The heart of each day's practice is the manifestation exercise. These exercises are designed to guide you through a specific activity that supports the day's theme. It could involve writing exercises, visualizations, affirmations, or deep reflections. The goal is to engage your mind, emotions, and energy so that you're actively participating in the manifestation process.

These exercises might ask you to:

- **Visualize your desires:** Imagine them in vivid detail, as though they've already come to life.
- **Write out your intentions:** Journaling helps clarify and solidify your desires in the physical realm.

- **Challenge your limiting beliefs:** Identifying and rewriting the negative thought patterns that might be holding you back.
- **Take inspired action:** Engage in practical steps that move you closer to your goals.

3. Action Step

While manifestation often involves inner work, it also requires action. At the end of each day, you may be encouraged to take small, inspired actions that align with your desires. These action steps are designed to move you forward, even if it's just one step at a time.

Remember, manifestation is not just about waiting for things to appear; it's about actively participating in the process and showing up for your dreams. Whether it's sending an email, making a phone call, or taking a moment to appreciate something you've manifested already, these actions help you stay in alignment with your desires.

4. Daily Affirmation or Mantra

To help anchor the energy of the day, you will be given a daily affirmation or mantra. Affirmations are powerful tools that reprogram your subconscious mind. By repeating these statements, you align your inner dialogue with the vibration of your desires. You are telling your mind that you believe in your ability to manifest and that you deserve the life you are calling in.
Each affirmation is carefully chosen to support the day's focus and help shift your mindset toward abundance, possibility, and confidence

Why 21 Days?

You may be wondering why this book is structured around 21 days. The number 21 is significant because it is commonly believed that it takes about three weeks to form a new habit, reprogram your subconscious, and shift your mindset. By committing to this practice every day for 21 days, you create a powerful shift in your energy, beliefs, and actions.

The Science and Spirit of 21 Days

From a neurological perspective, forming new habits and breaking old ones requires time and repetition. Studies suggest that consistent effort over 21 days can rewire neural pathways, creating new patterns of thought and behavior. Spiritually, this time frame represents a symbolic journey—a cycle of growth, intention, and alignment. It's long enough to create momentum but short enough to feel attainable.

During this time, you will be rewiring old habits, releasing limiting beliefs, and building new neural pathways that support your manifestation efforts. The consistency of showing up each day strengthens your ability to manifest and aligns your subconscious mind with your conscious desires.

Even if you miss a day or find yourself feeling discouraged at times, don't give up. Manifestation requires persistence and faith. If you miss a day, simply continue where you left off. Remember, this journey is about progress, not perfection.

How to Approach This Book

This book is designed to be a guide, but you are in control of how you approach it. While I suggest following the 21-day structure for maximum impact, feel free to adapt the exercises to suit your needs. The most important thing is to stay engaged and committed to the process, even if some days are more challenging than others.

Here are a few tips to help you make the most of your 21-day manifestation journey:

- Commit to the Process: Even on days when you feel like skipping, commit to doing something, even if it's just for a few minutes. Consistency is key.
- Stay Open: Manifestation works best when you approach it with an open mind and heart. Let go of any rigid expectations, and allow the process to unfold naturally.
- Take It at Your Own Pace: If you need to spend more time on a particular exercise or theme, feel free to do so. The journey is personal, and you can move through it at your own pace.
- Trust Yourself: You have everything you need within you to manifest your desires. Trust your intuition, and know that the universe is supporting you every step of the way

21 Days of Manifestation is a practical, powerful tool to help you create the life you desire. By engaging in daily practices, focusing on your intentions, and taking inspired action, you will shift your energy and align yourself with the abundant universe. This book is your guide, but you are the creator of your reality.

I am so excited to see what unfolds for you in the next 21 days. Let's begin this journey with an open heart, a focused mind, and the unwavering belief that your dreams are within reach.

The power to manifest your desires is already within you. Let's bring them into reality, one day at a time.

21 Days of Manifestation

Day 1

Preparation for Your Manifestation Journey

Welcome to the beginning of a transformative journey! Day 1 is all about preparation—clearing the physical, mental, and emotional clutter that may block your progress, and creating a space where your intentions can thrive. By dedicating time today to preparing your environment and inner world, you are signaling to the universe that you are ready to co-create the life you desire.

Clearing Your Space

Manifestation flourishes in a clean, clear space—both externally and internally. Imagine trying to grow a garden in soil filled with weeds. Similarly, your goals need a clutter-free environment to thrive. Today, you'll take steps to declutter both your physical surroundings and your inner world.

w

Exercise 1: Declutter Your Physical Space

1. **Choose a Space to Tidy:** This could be your desk, bedroom, or the area you plan to use as your manifestation corner.
2. **Remove What Doesn't Serve You:** Let go of items that no longer bring joy, serve a purpose, or inspire you.
3. **Organize and Refresh:** Arrange the remaining items neatly, and consider adding a touch of beauty—a candle, plant, or inspiring photo.

Exercise 2: Clear Your Mental and Emotional Space

1. **Journal Your Thoughts:** Write down any worries, doubts, or fears cluttering your mind.
2. **Release Through Intention:** Imagine placing these thoughts in a bubble and watching them float away. Say, "I release what no longer serves me."
3. **Practice Gratitude:** Write down three things you are grateful for to shift your energy into a higher vibration.

Raising Your Vibration

Your vibrational frequency determines the energy you send out to the universe. When you vibrate at a higher frequency—through love, joy, and gratitude—you attract similar high-frequency experiences.

Exercise 3: Discover Ways to Feel Happy and Joyful

Happiness and joy come from engaging in activities that bring you a sense of fulfillment and positivity. Taking time to indulge in simple pleasures can significantly enhance your mood and overall well-being. Here are some ways to cultivate joy in your daily life:

1. **Spend Time Outdoors:** Step outside and soak in the warmth of the sun and the freshness of the air. A walk in the park, a hike, or even sitting in a garden can bring relaxation and joy.
2. **Play and Interact:** Whether it's playing with children, engaging with your pet, or participating in fun group activities, playfulness fosters a sense of lightheartedness and happiness.

3. **Listen to Music:** Whether you enjoy calming melodies, energetic beats, or nostalgic tunes, listening to your favorite songs can bring immense pleasure and relaxation.
4. **Dance Freely:**You don't need to be a professional—simply moving to the rhythm of your favorite music can bring instant joy.

Learn to Meditate

Meditation is a powerful tool for raising your vibration and centering your thoughts

Exercise 4:

1. **Find a Quiet Spot:** Sit comfortably in your cleared space.
2. **Focus on Your Breath:** Inhale deeply for a count of four, hold for four, and exhale for four. Repeat this cycle for a few minutes.
3. **Visualize Calm:** Imagine a soft golden light surrounding you, filling you with peace and positivity.

Learn to Visualize

Visualization bridges the gap between your imagination and reality. When you see your desires as though they are already yours, you align your energy with them.

Exercise 5:

1. **Close Your Eyes:** Picture your life as if your desires have already manifested.
2. **Engage Your Senses:** Imagine how it looks, feels, sounds, and even smells.
3. **Feel the Emotion:** Let the joy, excitement, or gratitude of having your desires flow through you.

Sealing the Practice: Reflect, Recharge, and Reset

Day 1 is all about preparation—clearing space, setting intentions, and raising your vibration. These foundational steps are crucial for manifesting effectively. As you move through today, take pride in the effort you're investing in yourself and your dreams.

Tomorrow, we'll explore the art of visualization and how to use it to bring your desires to life. For now, trust that you've taken a powerful first step toward creating the reality you envision.

The universe is listening—let's continue to align with it.

"I am grateful for today and open to the abundance of tomorrow."

Day 2

Mastering the Art of Visualization for Manifestation

Visualization is a powerful tool in the manifestation process. It involves using your imagination to create a vivid mental image of your desires as if they have already materialized. This practice helps align your thoughts, emotions, and energy with your goals, bridging the gap between where you are and where you want to be. Mastering visualization Learning to visualize effectively can supercharge your manifestation efforts.

Why Visualization Works

Visualization taps into the power of the subconscious mind, which plays a crucial role in shaping your reality. By vividly imagining your desired outcomes, you:

- **Engage the Subconscious:** Your mind perceives these images as real, reinforcing beliefs and behaviors that support your goals.
- **Boost Emotional Alignment:** Feeling the emotions of success raises your vibration and aligns you with your desires.
- **Increase Focus:** A clear mental image keeps you motivated and helps you recognize and act on opportunities.

Exercise: Effective Visualization

1. Create a Focused Environment : Find a quiet, distraction-free space. Sit or lie down in a comfortable position, close your eyes, and take deep breaths to center yourself.

2. Define Your Vision : Be clear and specific about what you want to visualize. Consider:

- What does it look like?
- How does it feel?
- Who is involved?
- Where are you?

3. Engage Your Senses : Make your visualization immersive by incorporating all five senses. If visualizing a new home, imagine:

- The color of the walls
- The scent of fresh flowers
- The sound of laughter in the living room
- The softness of the carpets
- The taste of your favorite meal in the kitchen

4. Feel the Emotions : Emotions amplify manifestation. Feel the joy, excitement, and gratitude as if your goal has already been achieved.

5. Practice Consistently : Commit to 5–10 minutes of visualization daily. The best times are in the morning and before bed when the mind is most receptive.

Guided Visualization Exercise

1. Find a quiet space and close your eyes.
2. Take three deep breaths, inhaling calm and exhaling stress.

3. Imagine yourself achieving your goal. See the details, engage your senses, and immerse yourself in the emotions.
4. Stay in this state for a few minutes, then gently return to the present while holding onto the positive feelings.

Strengthening Your Visualization Skills

If you find it difficult to visualize, start small and train your mind like a muscle that needs strengthening.

Entering the Alpha State

The Alpha state is a relaxed mental state where brain wave patterns slow to 9-10 cycles per second. This pre-meditative state allows deeper access to the subconscious mind, making visualization more effective.

Begin with Simple Objects

If you're new to visualization, start with familiar, easy-to-reproduce images:

- A Lemon:
- Close your eyes and picture a bright yellow lemon.
- Feel its round shape in your hand.
- Imagine cutting it open and tasting its sourness.
- A Watermelon Slice:
- Visualize the deep green rind with bright red flesh and black seeds.
- Picture yourself holding it and tasting its sweet, juicy flavor.

Once you can clearly visualize simple objects, gradually move on to bigger goals and complex scenarios.

Sealing the Practice: Turning Vision into Reality

Visualization is a skill that strengthens with practice. By creating detailed mental images infused with positive emotions, you align yourself with the energy of your desires and bring them closer to reality. Incorporate this practice into your daily routine, and watch as your dreams unfold before you.

"I am grateful for the visions I've created today, knowing they are already on their way to me."

Day 3

Clarifying your desires

Welcome to Day 3 of your manifestation journey! Today, we dive into one of the most exciting and liberating parts of the process: **getting crystal clear about what you want.** Manifestation starts with clarity. You can't expect the universe to deliver your dreams if you're not even sure what they are! This is your opportunity to explore your desires unapologetically and embrace the limitless possibilities of what you can create.

Why Clarity Matters

Think of your desires like a destination on a map. If you don't know where you're going, how will you get there? Manifestation is no different. By defining what you want, you're giving the universe precise instructions to align circumstances, opportunities, and people to make your dreams a reality.

However, clarity isn't just for the universe—it's also for you. Knowing your desires helps you focus your energy, remove distractions, and stay aligned with your goals. This process is as much about self-discovery as it is about creating your dream life.

The Joy of Knowing What You Want

Today's task is all about indulging your desires without limitations. Think of this exercise as writing a wish list for Santa Claus—except Santa is the universe, and there are no rules about what you can ask for. Write a big fat list of what you want for christmas. Dig deep inside your life, mind and soul and bring out every known and unknown desire to mind. This is a space for pure, unfiltered desire. You're not being judged, and there's no penalty for dreaming big. The key is to focus on the what without worrying about the how or why—that part comes later.

Write It Down

Grab a notebook and let your imagination run wild. Writing your desires down helps solidify them in your mind and bridges the gap between thought and action. This is your Manifestation Journal you'll come back to every day. When you put pen to paper, you bring your dreams into the physical realm, making them more tangible and real. Here's how to approach it:

Exercise: Creating Your Wish List

1. Set the Scene: Go to your sacred spot. Light a candle or play soft music if it helps you relax.
2. Start with "I Want": Begin each sentence with "I want⊠" and let your desires flow.
3. Be Uninhibited: Write down anything and everything you want—big or small, material or emotional, simple or extravagant. Examples:
    - "I want to travel the world."
    - "I want a loving, fulfilling relationship."
    - "I want financial freedom."
    - "I want to wake up feeling healthy and energized every day."
4. Think Beyond the Material: While it's wonderful to want material things, also explore deeper desires: peace, joy, purpose, love, and connection.
5. Don't Overthink: Let this be a free-flowing exercise. There's no right or wrong desire.

Sealing the Practice: Permission to Dream

Day 3 is about permitting yourself to dream. By clarifying your desires, you are taking a powerful step toward manifesting them. Remember, there's no limit to what you can ask for or create. The universe is abundant, and so are you.

Tomorrow, we will dive deeper into 'Writing for Clarity' to transform your desires into actionable goals. For now, revel in the excitement of your dreams and trust that the universe is already conspiring in your favor.

Personal Perspective

When I first tried this exercise, I felt hesitant. Part of me thought, Is this silly? Do I even deserve to ask for all of this? But once I started writing, I realized how freeing it was to express my desires without judgment.

I wrote everything—some things practical (like a cozy home office), others wildly ambitious (like writing a bestselling book). What surprised me most was how good it felt to see all my dreams on paper. It gave me clarity, hope, and a sense of excitement about what was possible.

"I am worthy of every dream and desire. The universe supports me in creating the life I envision."

Day 4

From Desire to Goal-Clarifying Your Path

Welcome to Day 4 of your manifestation journey! After identifying your desires in Day 3, today is all about bringing structure and clarity to those dreams. Turning your desires into actionable goals is a powerful step that bridges the gap between what you want and how to achieve it. Writing for clarity helps you refine your focus, build confidence, and align your energy with the steps needed to manifest your vision. The most systematic way of clarifying desires is to divide our list into different categories that represent different aspects of our life, and start with our goals in each area.

When you write down your goals, you transform vague ideas into a tangible blueprint and shift from passive wishing to intentional action.

Steps to Clarify Your Desires

1. Reflect on Your True Desire

Before diving into goal-setting, take a moment to connect with your authentic self. Go through your list and ask yourself:

- Does it truly bring me joy?
- Does it fulfill me on a deeper level?
- Does it align with my values and purpose?
- Is this a want or a true need?

- Will this goal contribute to my long-term well-being and growth?

You might "want" a high-paying job, but what you truly "need" is a career that aligns with your values and offers creative fulfillment. This reflective process isn't about impressing others or conforming to external expectations. It's about uncovering what you genuinely want.

2. Write Down Your Desires as Goals

Turning desires into goals requires clarity and structure. Instead of vague aspirations, create specific and actionable statements.

Categorizing Your Goals

To effectively manifest your desires, begin by organizing your goals into key areas of life:

- Health
- Relationships
- Work/Career
- Wealth/Lifestyle
- Personal growth

For each category, take a moment to assess your current status and clarify where you aspire to be. Assign a score from **1 to 10** to reflect your satisfaction in each area, then establish a goal to elevate your score by at least one point.

Example:

- **Health** – Current Score: 4 | **Goal**: "Incorporate a 20-minute daily walk to enhance fitness and energy levels."
- **Relationships** – Current Score: 6 | **Goal**: "Dedicate one distraction-free evening per week to meaningful connection with my partner."

By setting clear, incremental goals, you create a structured path toward growth and alignment in all areas of your life.

Exercise:

1. In your Manifestation Journal, write down your current score for each category.
2. Identify 1-2 goals for each area that will take you to the next level.
3. Make sure your goals are specific, realistic, and aligned with your desires.

Personal Experience:
I remember rating my career a "5" because I felt stuck in a job that didn't inspire me. My goal was to explore freelance opportunities on weekends, which eventually led to a career change. Breaking it into small steps made the process less intimidating.

Sealing the Practice: Deepen Your Clarity and Focus

Day 4 is a powerful turning point in your manifestation journey. By reflecting on your true desires, differentiating between wants and needs, and writing down actionable goals, you create a roadmap for success. Remember, this is a process, not a race. Your clarity will deepen as you stay committed to your journey.

Tomorrow, we'll explore how to align your thoughts, emotions, and actions with your goals to amplify your manifestation power.

"Clarity flows through me, and I confidently create my reality."

Day 5

Writing for Creation-Manifestation Begins

Welcome to Day5! Now that you've clarified your desires and set actionable goals, it's time to take the next step in your manifestation journey: writing for creation. This practice goes beyond goal-setting; it transforms your intentions into powerful affirmations that resonate with the energy of having already achieved your desires. Writing in this way aligns your subconscious mind with the reality you're creating, bridging the gap between your current state and the life you envision.

Replace "Want" with "Have"

When you write your desires, express them in the present tense, as if they are already part of your life. This might feel strange or even unrealistic at first, but it's an essential step in the manifestation process. Words carry energy, and by speaking and writing as though you already have your desires, you create a vibrational match with the reality you're attracting.

Example Transformation:

- **Before:** "I want a fulfilling and exciting job."
- **After:** "I have a fulfilling and exciting job where I thrive, feel valued, and grow every day."

Personal Perspective:

I used to feel awkward writing about things I didn't yet

have as if they were real. But as I leaned into this practice, I noticed a shift. Writing in the present tense felt empowering, like stepping into a version of myself who already lived that life. Over time, this mindset fueled actions and decisions that brought me closer to those goals.

Define Your Desire

The more detailed you are, the clearer your signal to the universe. Think of the universe as a master artist waiting for you to provide a detailed sketch. The more parameters you define, the more aligned and precise your manifestation will be.

Questions to Guide You:

- What does this desire look like in detail?
- How does it make you feel?
- What are the key components of this goal?
- Who is involved, and where does this take place?
- What impact does this have on your life?

Exercise:

Write a detailed description of each goal as if you're painting a vivid picture. Include all the sensory details you can imagine.

Example:

Instead of saying, "I have a dream home," describe it:
"I live in a spacious, sunlit house with large windows overlooking the ocean. The scent of saltwater fills the air, and the sound of waves soothes me every morning. My kitchen is bright and modern, with marble countertops and cozy bar stools where my family gathers."

Sealing the Practice: Step into Creation

Today, you have moved from goal-setting to writing for creation—transforming desires into reality through present-tense writing. Your words create your world. Write with clarity and certainty, knowing each word shapes your future. l;paint vivid details, and feel the joy of already living your dreams.

"I am the creator of my reality. What I desire is already mine."

Day 6

Create a Vision – Envision Your Dream Life

Manifestation thrives on visualization. Today's practice is about immersing yourself in the imagery of your desired life and translating that vision into words.

Exercise 1: Meditative Visualization

1. Go to your sacred corner. Sit comfortably, close your eyes, and take a few deep breaths.
2. Picture yourself in the life you desire.
3. Observe every detail: the colors, sounds, textures, and even the scents around you.

Use all five senses.

- **Sight**: What do you see? The vibrant colors of a garden? The sleek design of your car?
- **Sound**: What do you hear? Laughter, music, or the hum of success?
- **Smell**: Can you smell freshly brewed coffee in your dream kitchen or the flowers in your backyard?
- **Touch**: What textures do you feel—soft fabrics, warm sunlight, or a cool breeze?
- **Taste**: Imagine savoring a meal in your dream home or sipping champagne to celebrate a success.

4. Step into the scene like you're watching a 3D movie where you're the star. Visualize the joy, ease, and fulfillment you feel in that moment.

Exercise 2: Write Your Vision

After your visualization, write down every detail as vividly as possible. Describe the scene in present tense, as if you're narrating a moment in your current life.

Example Vision Writing:

"I wake up in my dream home, sunlight streaming through the sheer curtains. The sound of birds chirping mixes with the gentle crash of waves outside. As I step onto the balcony, I feel the warmth of the sun on my face and the cool breeze from the ocean. My journal and morning coffee are waiting for me at the cozy nook I've created, where I feel inspired to write every day."

Sealing the Practice: Visualize, Write, and Watch Your Dreams Unfold

Day 4 and Day 5 are about stepping fully into your creative power. Writing and visualization work hand in hand, activating both your logical and imaginative sides. The more vividly you see and describe your desires, the more real they become—not just in your mind, but in your life.

As you move forward, revisit your writings and visualizations regularly. Let them inspire your daily actions and remind you of the incredible life you are manifesting. The universe is listening, and with every word and image, you're shaping your future.

"I see my desires clearly, and they are already manifesting in my life."

Day 7

Live the Feeling – Embody Your Desired Reality

•••
••

Welcome to Day 7 of your manifestation journey! Today's task is to move beyond the physical details of your desire and connect deeply with the emotion associated with it. Emotions are the fuel that drives the manifestation process. When you can embody the feelings of already having your desires, you align yourself with the vibrational frequency needed to attract them into your reality.

Exercise: Feel the Emotion of Your Desired Reality

You've already spent time visualizing and writing about your goals, but today is about truly **feeling** what it would be like to already have everything you desire. Sometimes, we may not have the exact clarity on the physical details of our desires, but we can always access how we want to feel. For example, you may not know exactly what your dream home looks like, but you may know that you want to feel **peaceful, safe, abundant**, or **joyful** there. It's important to connect with those feelings today.

1. Immerse Yourself in the Feeling

Go back to the vision you created yesterday. This time, instead of focusing purely on the details, pay close attention to how **you feel** in that scenario. Imagine yourself fully immersed in your desired reality, living it in the present moment.

- What emotions do you experience when you step into this life that you've manifested?
- Are you feeling **happy, fulfilled, excited, grateful**, or **proud**?
- Are you experiencing **calm**, **contentment**, or **security**?

2. Amplify the Feeling

Once you have identified the emotions associated with your desired reality, **amplify them**. Let the feelings **consume you** completely. Imagine the joy, the peace, the excitement in your body. Feel them in every cell, in every breath, in every pore of your being.

If you're visualizing yourself in your dream home, for instance, focus on how it feels to be there.

- "I feel peaceful and calm in my new home, surrounded by beauty and harmony."
- "I feel secure and confident, knowing I've created this life for myself."
- "I feel proud of how far I've come and the life I've manifested."

3. Bask in the glow of these feelings the whole day.

Sealing the Practice: Live the Feeling, Create the Reality

Day 7 is all about cultivating the emotional energy of your desired reality. By feeling the emotions of your desires, you are already living in the energy of your manifestations. When you align your emotions with your desires, you're giving the universe clear instructions on what you want. Keep practicing this feeling daily, and watch how your reality begins to shift in magical ways.

Tomorrow, we'll move on to creating your vision board, which will serve as a powerful visual reminder of the life you're manifesting! Keep the emotions flowing and let them guide you to your dreams.

"I embrace the emotions of love, prosperity, and happiness daily."

Day 8

Create a Vision Board – Visualize Your Desired Reality

Welcome to Day 8 of your manifestation journey! Today's task is to Create a Vision board A vision board is a powerful tool for manifestation that visually represents your goals and desires. By combining images, words, and symbols, a vision board helps you focus your energy, inspire creativity, and align your mindset with your aspirations. It serves as a daily reminder of your dreams and reinforces the belief that they are attainable.

Exercise: Create a Vision Board

1: Gather Your Supplies

You will need:

- A quiet, relaxed space where you can focus
- A board (corkboard, poster board, or digital canvas for online vision boards)
- Scissors, glue, or push pins
- Magazines, printed images, or digital visuals
- Markers, stickers, or decorative materials

2: Reflect on Your Goals and Desires

Take time to think about what you want to manifest in different areas of your life, such as:

- Career and finances
- Health and well-being

- Relationships
- Personal growth
- Travel and experiences

Read these goals from your Journal to gain clarity and intention before selecting visuals.

3: Choose Meaningful Images and Words

Find pictures, phrases, and symbols that resonate with your desires. For example:

- If you want financial abundance, use images of money, successful business icons, or luxury items.
- For health goals, include pictures of vibrant foods, exercise equipment, or serene nature scenes.

4: Arrange and Assemble

Lay out your images and words on the board before securing them. Arrange them in a way that feels intuitive and inspiring to you. Group related items together or create distinct sections for each life area. As you do this, take a moment to **visualize** each image coming into your reality.

5: Add Personal Touches

Incorporate personal affirmations, quotes, or handwritten notes to make the board uniquely yours. Use colors and decorations that evoke positive emotions. This is your board, so make it **personal** and aligned with your unique desires.

6: Display Your Vision Board

Once your vision board is complete, place it somewhere you can see it every day. The goal is to make it a constant reminder of what you're manifesting. Whether it's in your bedroom, office, living room, or your computer screen, seeing your vision board daily will help you stay connected to your desires and remind you of the goals you're working toward. Spend a few minutes each day focusing on your board. Visualize yourself achieving your goals and feel the emotions associated with success.

Sealing the Practice: Let Your Vision Guide You

Day 8 is a fun and creative task that will serve as a constant reminder of your desires and goals. By creating a vision board, you are physically manifesting your desires through imagery and emotion. Remember, a vision board isn't just a collage of pretty pictures—it's a visual representation of the life you're actively creating. The more you connect with the emotions tied to those images, the more aligned you will become with the universe's ability to bring them into your reality.

Tomorrow, we'll continue on our journey with more powerful practices to keep your manifestation energy flowing. Keep the excitement alive and stay inspired by your vision!

"I see it, I feel it, and it's already mine."

Day 9

Release and Receive

Welcome to Day 9 of your manifestation journey! Today we are going toRelease and receive. Letting go of attachment to your desires is a crucial step in the manifestation process. Holding on too tightly to your goals can create resistance and block the flow of energy needed to bring them into reality. Letting go does not mean giving up; it means trusting the process, releasing control, and allowing the universe to work its magic.

The Exercise: "Release and Trust Ritual"

This simple yet powerful exercise will guide you in letting go of your desire while maintaining positive intention and trust.

1: Create a Calm Space

Step into Your Sacred Space. Light a candle or play soothing music if it helps you relax. Bring your journal and a pen along.

2: Write Down Your Desire

On a piece of paper or in your journal, write your desire in a positive and present-tense statement. For example:

- "I am living in financial abundance."
- "I am in a loving, supportive relationship."

As you write, focus on the emotions you feel when your desire is fulfilled—joy, peace, gratitude, or excitement.

3: Reflect on Your Intention

Take a moment to reflect on why this desire is important to you. Acknowledge its significance and express gratitude for the possibility of it becoming reality.

4: Visualize Letting It Go

Close your eyes and take a few deep breaths. Imagine holding your desire in your hands as a glowing light or tangible object. Visualize yourself gently releasing it into the universe, watching it float away, carried by the wind or into a stream of light. As you do, affirm:

- "I release my desire with love and trust."
- "I know the universe is working on my behalf."
- "I trust the process and know everything is unfolding perfectly."
- "I am open to receiving my desires in divine timing."
- "I release attachment and embrace faith."

Sealing the Practice: Trust, Surrender, Receive

Today's task of letting go is a crucial step in the manifestation process. It's not about abandoning your desires, it's about releasing the need to control the outcome and trusting that the universe will bring everything you've asked for in its own time and way. By embracing surrender and detachment, you open up space for greater possibilities and invite more ease and flow into your life.

I encourage you to practice letting go not just today, but every day. The more you trust the process, the more you'll see how beautifully the universe aligns things for you.

Remember, your desires are already on their way. All you need to do is believe, trust, and surrender.

"I release the need to control outcomes and embrace the flow of life."

Day 10

Gratitude – The Bridge to Manifestation

Welcome to Day 10 of your manifestation journey! Today, we focus on one of the most transformative and powerful tools for manifesting your desires. Gratitude is the bridge between where you are now and where you want to be. It aligns your vibration with abundance and strengthens your connection to the universe.

When you are grateful, you acknowledge the blessings in your life, creating an energetic state of positivity, which attracts more to be grateful for. Gratitude isn't just about thanking the universe for what you have; it's also about expressing thanks for the things you're manifesting, as if they've already arrived.

Step 1: Morning Gratitude Practice

Start your day by listing things you're grateful for. This simple act sets a positive tone for the rest of the day.

Exercise: Morning Gratitude Journal

1. Grab your journal and write down 5-10 things you're grateful for.
   - Examples: "I'm grateful for my supportive friends," or "I'm grateful for the opportunities that come my way."
2. Focus on specific details. For example, instead of saying, "I'm grateful for my home," try, "I'm grateful for the

warmth and comfort of my home, where I feel safe and secure."

3. As you write, pause and feel the gratitude in your heart. Visualize each blessing and let the feeling expand within you.

Step 2: Gratitude for What You're Manifesting

Gratitude becomes even more powerful when you express it for the things you're manifesting. By doing this, you align with the energy of already having them.

Exercise: Future Gratitude Statements

1. Write a list of things you're manifesting as if they've already come to pass.
   Examples:
- "I'm so grateful for my fulfilling new job where I feel valued and inspired every day."
- "I'm so thankful for the beautiful home I now live in, surrounded by love and peace."
2. Repeat these statements daily, feeling the emotions of gratitude as if your desires are already part of your life.

Step 3: Evening Reflection

Before bed, take a moment to reflect on your day and identify moments of gratitude. This practice helps you end your day on a positive note and primes your subconscious mind for abundance.

Exercise: Evening Gratitude Reflection

1. Write down 3-5 things that happened during the day that you're grateful for.
- Examples: "I'm grateful for the smile from a stranger," or "I'm thankful for the peaceful walk I took in the evening."

2. Reflect on what went well, no matter how small, and allow yourself to feel appreciation.

Step 4: Gratitude Meditation

Meditation amplifies gratitude by allowing you to connect deeply with your emotions and the present moment.

Exercise: Gratitude Meditation

1. Sit in your sacred space and close your eyes.
2. Take a few deep breaths and focus on your heart.
3. Visualize moments, people, or experiences you're grateful for. Imagine a warm, golden light expanding in your chest with each thought.
4. End your meditation by silently or aloud saying, "Thank you. Thank you. Thank you."

Sealing the Practice: Gratitude for Today, Abundance for Tomorrow

Gratitude is the key that unlocks the door to abundance. By appreciating what you have and expressing gratitude for what's coming, you align yourself with the energy of receiving. This powerful practice not only amplifies your manifestation efforts but also enriches your everyday life.

Remember, gratitude is more than a step in the manifestation process—it's a lifestyle. As you cultivate gratitude daily, you'll notice how your perspective shifts and how the universe responds by bringing more blessings into your life.

Let gratitude guide you today and every day!

"I am deeply grateful for all that I have and all that is on its way to me."

Day 11

Inspired Action

Welcome to Day 11 of your manifestation journey! Today's task isAfter setting your desire into motion, remain open to taking action—but not through force or endless effort. Inspired action arises naturally, often as an intuitive nudge, a deep knowing, or an unexpected opportunity that feels exciting and aligned.

While logic and planning have their place, true manifestation taps into a deeper intelligence—your subconscious mind—which guides you through intuition, gut feelings, and synchronicities. Like driving at night with headlights, you may not see the full path, but by trusting your inner GPS, you'll always be led in the right direction.

Today, tune in, trust, and act on your intuitive guidance.

Exercise1 : Tune into Your Inner Guidance

1. Begin the day by setting an intention: "I am open to receiving inspired action today."
2. Take a few deep breaths, close your eyes, and ask yourself: "What is one small action I can take today that aligns with my desires?"
3. Notice any thoughts, feelings, or sensations that arise—these may be clues from your intuition.

Exercise 2: Take Inspired Action

1. Be aware of subtle nudges throughout the day. It might

be an idea that pops into your mind, a strong feeling to reach out to someone, or an unexpected opportunity presenting itself.

2. Trust the guidance and take at least one action—no matter how small. This could be:
   - Sending an email or message to someone who comes to mind.
   - Changing your routine in a way that feels inspired.
   - Researching a topic that sparks excitement.
   - Taking a spontaneous walk or visiting a new place.
3. The key is to act without overthinking or doubting—just follow the energy of excitement or curiosity.

Exercise 3: Reflect and Notice Synchronicities

1. At the end of the day, journal about your experience:
   - What action did you take?
   - How did it feel? Did it feel effortless, exciting, or aligned?
   - Did anything unexpected happen as a result?
2. Often, inspired action leads to synchronicities—signs that you are on the right path. Be on the lookout for meaningful coincidences, unexpected opportunities, or moments of clarity.

The more you practice taking action from intuition rather than fear or logic alone, the more effortlessly the universe will guide you toward your manifestations. Inspired action is not about struggle—it's about flow, trust, and alignment.

Sealing the Practice: Trust and Take the Next Step

Taking inspired action is about trusting your inner guidance and following the gentle nudges from the universe. With every aligned step, you move closer to your desires. Inspired action flows with ease and joy. It's not about effort; it's about following the energy that feels exciting and right. Trust that you don't need to see the whole path—each inspired action lights the way. Keep trusting your inner GPS and take inspired steps every day, knowing that each action brings you closer to your dreams.Stay open, curious, and courageous. The universe is always guiding you.

"I trust my inner guidance and take inspired action with ease and confidence."

Day 12

Give What You Want – Creating an Abundant Flow

Welcome to Day 12 of your manifestation journey! Today, we explore a powerful yet often overlooked principle of manifestation: the act of giving. What you put out into the universe creates an energetic flow that mirrors your desires. By giving what you want to receive, you align yourself with abundance, creating a reciprocal loop of energy that accelerates manifestation. Acts of giving naturally generate feelings of joy, gratitude, and connection—powerful emotional states for manifesting.

The Energy of Giving

When you give freely, you're signaling to the universe that you already have abundance. This shifts your energy from a place of lack to one of fulfillment and generosity. For example, if you desire love, offering kindness and care to others creates a vibration that attracts more love into your life.

How to Practice Giving

You don't have to give in grand ways. The intention behind your actions matters more than the scale.

Exercise: Giving with Intention

1: Give What You Want

- Choose one area of life where you want to manifest abundance (e.g., love, money, health, success). How can you offer that same energy to others?

- Write down three small, meaningful ways you can give in this area.
- Want more love? Offer genuine compliments, listen actively, or express affection to someone you care about.
- Want financial abundance? Donate a small amount to charity, buy coffee for a friend, or share a resource with someone in need.
- Want success? Offer mentorship or encouragement to someone pursuing their goals.
- Pick one of these actions and carry it out with a heart full of gratitude and joy.

2: Give Your Time and Energy
Giving doesn't always involve money or material things. Sharing your time, attention, or skills can be just as impactful. For example, volunteering for a cause you care about or helping a friend in need can create powerful energy shifts.

3: Practice Random Acts of Kindness
Spontaneous generosity creates ripples of positivity. Pay for someone's coffee, leave an encouraging note for a coworker, or simply smile at a stranger.

Sealing the Practice: "Sow Generosity, Reap Abundance"

Day 12 is about becoming the energy you wish to attract. Every act of giving sends a ripple into the universe. When you give with intention, you not only uplift others but also elevate your own vibration. Over time, you'll notice how these small acts of generosity return to you in ways that often exceed your expectations.

Remember, giving doesn't have to be extravagant—what matters is the authenticity and love behind your actions. The universe responds to this energy with equal generosity, ensuring that what you put out will return to you multiplied.

Tomorrow, we'll explore how to navigate doubts and strengthen your belief in the manifestation process. For now, focus on giving from the heart and watch as the energy you release begins to flow back to you.

"I give freely and receive abundantly."

Day 13

Breakthrough Time - Removing Manifestation Blocks

“Let Go of Limiting Beliefs"

Welcome to Day 13 of your manifestation journey! The outcome is a result of our frequency alignment with our desires. Our thoughts and emotions shape our frequency, but deep-rooted subconscious patterns—our beliefs—often pull us back to old ways of thinking, preventing alignment with what we want to manifest. Today, we'll focus on addressing the mental blocks that hinder the manifestation process.

To begin with, we'll focus on identifying and releasing these hidden beliefs and energies. Some of them are so deeply embedded in our subconscious that we may not even realize they exist. This exercise will help you bring those beliefs to light, challenge them, and replace them with empowering ones that support your manifestation journey.

Once you clear the mental and emotional clutter, you create space for higher-vibrational energies—such as love, faith, and abundance—to flow freely. These higher frequencies attract the experiences and desires you seek.

Tomorrow, we'll take this work further by shifting to the etheric plane. We'll focus on releasing energetic blocks and aligning your vibration with your desires to complete this powerful manifestation process.

Checking Beliefs: The Hidden Saboteurs

Our beliefs shape our reality. If you hold subconscious

beliefs that contradict your desires, they can interfere with your manifestation process. For example:

- Desire: Financial abundance.
- Limiting Belief: "Money is hard to come by" or "I don't deserve wealth."

Exercise

1: Identify Your Limiting Beliefs

Write down your current desires. Then, reflect on any doubts, fears, or "yeah, but⊠" thoughts that arise. Ask yourself:

- What thoughts or doubts arise when I think about achieving this goal?
- Are there recurring negative statements I tell myself about this desire?
- Where might these beliefs have originated (past experiences, societal norms, or upbringing)?

Write down all the limiting beliefs that come to mind, such as, "I don't deserve success" or "I'm not good enough." Be as honest and thorough as possible.

2: Question the Beliefs

Choose one limiting belief at a time and ask yourself:

- Is this belief absolutely true?
- What evidence do I have that contradicts this belief?
- How has this belief held me back in the past?
- What would my life look like without this belief?

By questioning your limiting beliefs, you weaken their hold on your subconscious mind.

3: Reframe the Beliefs

Rewrite each limiting belief into a positive, empowering affirmation. For example:

- Limiting Belief: "I don't deserve success."
- Empowering Belief: "I am deserving of success and all the good things life has to offer."

Write your new beliefs in the present tense, focusing on what you want to believe and feel.

4: Visualize Your Empowered Self

Close your eyes and visualize yourself living in alignment with your new, empowering beliefs. Imagine the confidence, joy, and success you experience as these beliefs shape your reality. Feel the emotions as vividly as possible.

Sealing the Practice: "From Limitation to Liberation"

Removing limiting beliefs is a powerful step toward manifesting your desires. By identifying, challenging, and reframing these beliefs, you open yourself to greater possibilities and align your mindset with the energy of abundance and success. Make this practice a regular part of your manifestation journey to unlock your full potential.

"I release limiting beliefs and embrace infinite possibilities."

Day 14

Removing Manifestation Blocks - 2
Energy Clearing

The mental blocks that we have been working on since yesterday, are not just fleeting thoughts; they are energetic imprints. Negative energies—whether rooted in past experiences, deep-seated fears, or limiting beliefs—act like dense clouds in your energetic field, obstructing the natural flow of manifestation. These energies vibrate at a lower frequency, anchoring you in cycles of fear, scarcity, self-doubt, and unworthiness. Left unchecked, they disrupt the free flow of abundance, joy, and love that is meant for you.

Beliefs, much like thoughts, are energy patterns that take form through repetition. These patterns become stored in your etheric energy body. The empowering truth is that these energetic imprints can be cleared. By releasing and cleansing these stagnant energies, you raise your vibration to a higher frequency—one that aligns with love, abundance, and joy. As your frequency rises, you naturally attract the reality that matches it, effortlessly drawing in the experiences, relationships, and opportunities that resonate with your highest intentions and desires.

How to Identify and Clear Negative Energies

Energy Clearing Practices

- **Meditation**: Visualize a bright, cleansing light washing over you, dissolving any negative energies.
- **Smudging**: Use sage, palo santo, or incense to clear stagnant energy from your physical space.

- **Salt Bath**: Take a bath with Epsom or Himalayan salt to detoxify and cleanse your aura.
- **Sound Healing:** Listen to high-vibrational music or use a singing bowl to clear energetic blockages.

Exercise: The Violet Light Technique

This powerful exercise helps you clear limiting beliefs and energetically align with your desired manifestation.

1: Identify Your Goal
Choose one significant goal you wish to manifest.

2: Reveal Limiting Beliefs

- Visualize a large whiteboard in front of you.
- Write down your goal at the top.
- Now, begin listing all the reasons—both conscious and subconscious—why you believe you cannot achieve this goal. Dig deep and allow any doubts, fears, or past conditioning to surface.

3: Clear the Blocks

- Imagine a violet-light eraser in your hand.
- One by one, erase each limiting belief from the board. As you do, visualize the negative energy dissolving, freeing your mind and energy field from these blocks.

4: Affirm Your Desire

- With a clear board, rewrite your goal in the present tense, as if it is already yours.
- Describe it vividly, incorporating sensory details—how it looks, feels, and impacts your life.
- Immerse yourself in the emotions of already having it—joy, gratitude, excitement.

This is more than just a symbolic exercise. Limiting beliefs are dense, stagnant energy that can block the natural flow of abundance. By consciously identifying and releasing them, you create space for new, empowering energy to take root, allowing your desires to manifest with greater ease

Sealing the Practice: "Releasing to Rise"

Day 14 is about taking a courageous step inward. By clearing negative energies and examining your beliefs, you are creating a space for positivity and abundance to flourish. Cleaning negative energy is not about perfection—it's a gradual process of awareness and release. With each step, you'll feel lighter, more empowered, and more aligned with your goals.

Tomorrow, we'll explore how to strengthen your connection with the universe and trust the timing of your manifestations. For now, focus on releasing what no longer serves you and embracing beliefs that empower your journey.

"With each release, I invite powerful, vibrant possibilities into my life."

Day 15

Fire Ritual

Welcome to Day 15 of your manifestation journey! Today, we're tapping into the ancient and transformative power of a **fire ritual**. Fire represents cleansing, release, and creation. This ritual is a symbolic way to let go of what no longer serves you, clear energetic blocks, and make space for new possibilities to flow into your life.

Why the Fire Ritual Works

The fire ritual works on multiple levels:

1. Emotional Release: Burning what holds you back helps release the energy tied to negative emotions or limiting beliefs.
2. Symbolic Closure: It provides a physical act that represents the end of old cycles and the beginning of new ones.
3. Manifestation Amplifier: Fire is a dynamic, transformative force that symbolizes action and creation, helping to fuel your intentions.

Exercise: Fire Ritual

1. Set Your Intention

- Reflect on what you want to release: fears, doubts, limiting beliefs, negative patterns, or past experiences.
- Identify the emotions or situations that are no longer serving your growth.

2. Write It Down

- On a piece of paper, write down everything you wish to let go of. Be specific.
- Examples:
  - "I release my fear of failure."
  - "I let go of resentment toward [name]."
  - "I release the belief that I am not worthy of success."

3. Create a Sacred Space

- Find a safe, quiet place where you can perform the ritual without disturbance.
- Gather materials:
  - A fireproof container (like a metal bowl or fireplace)
  - Matches or a lighter
  - Optional: Candles, crystals, or calming music to set the mood

4. Perform the Ritual

- Light a candle or create a small, contained fire in your fireproof container.
- Take a deep breath and focus on your intention to release.
- One by one, place the pieces of paper into the fire and watch them burn.
- As the flames consume the paper, imagine the energy of what you're releasing being transformed and carried away.
- Repeat affirmations such as:
  - "I release this with love and gratitude."
  - "I am free from what no longer serves me."
  - "I create space for new blessings to enter my life."

5. Close the Ritual

- Once all the paper is burned, take a moment to sit

quietly.

- Reflect on the lightness you feel and the new space you've created within yourself.
- If possible, bury or scatter the ashes as a final act of letting go.

Personal Perspective: My Experience with the Fire Ritual

The first time I performed a fire ritual, I was amazed at how cathartic it felt. Writing down my fears and doubts made them tangible, and watching them burn gave me a profound sense of relief. One of the things I released was my fear of speaking up. I felt a weight lifted as the flames consumed that fear, and soon after, I found myself naturally more confident in conversations.The fire ritual has become a cherished practice for me, one I revisit whenever I feel stuck or need a fresh start. It reminds me that transformation often requires letting go and trusting in the power of renewal.

Sealing the Practice:

Engaging in a fire ritual offers a profound method to release what no longer serves you, making way for new opportunities. By writing down your fears and doubts and then burning them, you transform intangible concerns into tangible actions, leading to a significant sense of relief and renewal. This symbolic act of burning away the old creates energetic space for your dreams to flourish, embodying the transformative power of letting go and embracing new beginnings.

"I release all that no longer serves me and welcome new beginnings."

Day 16

Create A Wholesome Life

Just as we take the time to clean and enhance every space in our home, we must also nurture and refine each area of our lives. True success is not defined by achievements in a single aspect but by a sense of balance and fulfillment across all areas. A truly successful life is one where health, relationships, career, and personal well-being are in harmony.

Over the next few days, we will focus on different aspects of life, setting clear intentions and manifesting meaningful goals in each area. This holistic approach will help you create lasting transformation and alignment with your highest potential.

Focus on Health

Welcome to Day 16 of your manifestation journey! Today, we turn our attention to one of the most vital aspects of creating your dream life: your health. Physical, mental, and emotional well-being form the foundation for everything you wish to manifest. By prioritizing your health, you align your energy with vitality and abundance, making it easier to attract your desires.

Exercise: Manifest Better Health

1. Set a Health Intention

- Reflect on your current state of health. What areas

need more attention?
- Set a clear intention for improvement.
- Examples:
    - "I am nourishing my body with wholesome foods."
    - "I choose daily movement to keep my body strong."
    - "I prioritize rest and relaxation to rejuvenate my mind and spirit

2. Use Affirmations for Health

- Affirmations can rewire your mindset and reinforce your commitment to health.
- Examples:
    - "I am healthy, strong, and full of energy."
    - "My body knows how to heal and restore itself."
    - "I choose habits that support my well-being."

3. Visualize Optimal Health

- Sit in a quiet space and visualize yourself in peak health.
- Imagine the vitality in your body, the clarity in your mind, and the joy in your spirit.
- Feel the energy of good health radiating through every cell of your being.

4. Take Inspired Action

- Small, consistent actions can make a big difference in your overall well-being. Choose one or two actions to focus on today:
- **Physical Health:**
    - Drink more water.
    - Prepare a healthy meal or snack.
    - Move your body through yoga, walking, or another enjoyable activity.

- **Mental Health:**
    - Practice deep breathing exercises or mindfulness meditation.
    - Limit time spent on devices and reconnect with nature.
- **Emotional Health:**
    - Journal about your emotions and release any pent-up feelings.
    - Spend time with loved ones who uplift and inspire you.

Sealing the Practice: Anchoring Health Habits

Your health is the cornerstone of your manifestation journey. By taking small, intentional steps to care for your body, mind, and spirit, you align yourself with the energy of vitality and abundance. Remember, prioritizing your well-being isn't selfish—it's essential. When you feel your best, you can give your best to the world.

"My body vibrates with energy and health."

Day 17

Create a wholesome life-
Focus on Relationships

Welcome to Day 17 of your manifestation journey! Today, we dive into one of the most important areas of life—relationships. Whether it's your relationship with a romantic partner, family, friends, or even yourself, healthy, nurturing relationships are key to creating a fulfilling life. Relationships significantly impact your energy, emotions, and ability to manifest your desires.

Why Focus on Relationships?

1. **Emotional Support:** Positive relationships provide the emotional foundation you need to stay motivated and resilient.
2. **Shared Energy:** Relationships can amplify or drain your energy, so surrounding yourself with positive people can elevate your vibration.
3. **Manifesting Love:** Whether you want to strengthen existing relationships or attract new ones, the energy you put out into the world plays a major role in the relationships you attract.

Exercise: Manifest Healthy Relationships

1. Set Your Intention for Relationship Manifestation

- Reflect on the type of relationship you want to manifest.
- **Romantic:** Are you looking for a soulmate or wanting to deepen your connection with a partner?

- **Friendship:** Are you craving deeper, more meaningful friendships?
- **Family**: Do you want to heal or strengthen bonds with family members?
- Write down your relationship goals and set a clear intention.
- Examples:
- "I attract loving, supportive, and healthy relationships into my life."
- "I communicate openly and honestly with those I care about."
- "I am worthy of deep, meaningful connections."

2. Reflect on the Relationships You Currently Have

- Take a moment to think about your existing relationships—what's working and what's not?
- Are there any patterns, limiting beliefs, or past wounds that are holding you back from having the kinds of relationships you desire?
- Consider journaling about how you feel in your relationships and how you'd like them to evolve.

3: Envision Your Ideal Relationship

Imagine yourself surrounded by love, warmth, and harmony. If you're manifesting a new relationship, visualize yourself with a partner who truly understands and supports you. Picture their kindness, laughter, and the deep connection you share. Feel the emotions of love, security, and joy as if this relationship already exists in your life.

If you're working on an existing relationship, visualize positive interactions with this person. See yourself having heartfelt conversations, sharing joyful moments, and resolving any past misunderstandings with grace and compassion. Imagine both of you embracing a new level of understanding and closeness.

4: Engage All Your Senses

Make the visualization as vivid as possible:

- See the smiles, the affectionate gestures, the deep eye contact.
- Hear the laughter, the kind words, the meaningful conversations.
- Feel the warmth of a hug, the joy of connection, and the deep sense of belonging.

The more real it feels, the more powerfully you align with this reality.

5: Radiate Love and Gratitude

Now, imagine your heart filling with love and gratitude. See this energy expanding outward, touching every relationship in your life. Send appreciation for the love you already have and trust that even greater connections are manifesting.

Affirm to yourself:
"I am worthy of deep, loving, and fulfilling relationships. Love flows effortlessly into my life. My relationships are built on trust, joy, and mutual understanding."

6. Improve Your Relationship with Yourself

Before attracting or improving external relationships, the relationship you have with yourself is the foundation. Self-love and self-respect are essential.

- Take time today to nurture yourself—whether it's through meditation, self-care rituals, or simply being kind to yourself.
- Affirmations for self-love:
    - "I am deserving of love, respect, and understanding."
    - "I honor and appreciate myself fully."
    - "I attract healthy and loving relationships

because I love and respect myself."

7. Take Inspired Action

Relationships require action. What's one thing you can do today to strengthen or deepen a relationship?

- Send a loving message or reach out to someone you've been meaning to connect with.
- Express appreciation for the people in your life.
- If you're looking to manifest a new relationship, take steps to meet new people or explore opportunities to connect.

Personal Perspective: My Journey with Relationships

For me, focusing on relationships was a pivotal moment in my manifestation journey. I realized that in order to manifest deep, meaningful connections, I needed to first cultivate a loving relationship with myself. When I began nurturing myself, setting boundaries, and prioritizing self-love, I noticed how my interactions with others shifted.

One simple change I made was to practice gratitude for my existing relationships, even the small ones. This shift in energy helped me attract more love, care, and understanding into my life. I also started reaching out more often to my friends and family, showing them appreciation in ways I hadn't before. And the best part? My relationships flourished, becoming more authentic and enriching.

Sealing the Practice: Building Strong, Loving Relationships

Healthy, loving relationships are essential for your personal growth and manifestation journey. By setting clear intentions, working on self-love, and practicing gratitude, you create a magnetic energy that attracts the right people into your life. Remember, the love and connection you seek in others begin within yourself.

Tomorrow, we will focus on **manifesting wealth and abundance**. But for today, nurture the relationships around you and watch as they evolve into the supportive, loving connections you deserve.

"I attract trusting and loving relationships."

Day 18

Creating a wholesome life
Focus on Work/Career

Welcome to Day 18! Today, we are diving deep into the area of work and career. This is an area where many of us spend a significant amount of time, and it plays a major role in shaping our lives. Whether you're looking for a new job, wanting to elevate your current career, or seeking fulfillment and passion in your work, the energy you put into manifesting your ideal career will greatly affect your success.

Why Focus on Career Manifestation?

1. **Financial Stability:** A fulfilling career brings financial security and the freedom to live your desired lifestyle.
2. **Personal Fulfillment:** A career that aligns with your passions and values brings personal satisfaction and a sense of purpose.
3. **Growth & Expansion:** Your career can be a source of personal growth, learning, and the opportunity to make a positive impact on the world.

EXERCISE: Manifest a Successful Career1. Clarify Your Career Goals

The first step in manifesting your ideal career is to be clear about what you want. This clarity will direct your energy and actions towards the career you desire.

- What is your ideal career?
- Do you want to grow in your current role, shift industries, or start your own business?

1: Write down your career goals and intentions.

- Examples:
    - "I am doing meaningful work that aligns with my values."
    - "I am attracting new opportunities that bring growth and fulfillment."
    - "I am excelling in my career and being recognized for my efforts."

2: Visualize Your Ideal Work Life

Visualization is one of the most powerful tools for manifesting your career goals. Spend time today visualizing your perfect work situation.

- Imagine yourself in your dream job, whether it's in your current company or a new role.
- Picture yourself waking up excited to go to work, engaging in work that you love, and receiving the rewards for your effort.
- Engage all your senses to make the vision feel real. What does your office look like? What's the energy like in your workspace? How does it feel to succeed?

3: Identify Your Skills & Strengths

Recognizing your skills and strengths will help you focus on what you bring to the table. It will also provide you with the confidence to step into your desired role.

- Reflect on what you excel at in your career.
- What are your natural talents?
- What skills do you want to develop or improve upon?
- Write down your skills and strengths. Consider how you can enhance them to align with your career goals.

4: Overcome Limiting Beliefs

If there are any limiting beliefs or doubts about your career, today is the day to confront them. These beliefs might be holding you back from pursuing your true potential.

- Ask yourself:
  - What beliefs do I have about my career?
  - Do I feel worthy of success and fulfillment in my work?
  - What are the fears or doubts that come up when I think about my career?
- Write these limiting beliefs down and then rewrite them into empowering beliefs.
  - Example: "I am not good enough for this job" becomes "I have all the skills I need to succeed and grow in my career."
  - Example: "I can't make a living doing what I love" becomes "I am attracting abundance by doing meaningful work."

5: Take Inspired Action Toward Your Career Goals

Manifestation requires action. Even if it's just a small step, take inspired action toward your career goals today.

- This might include updating your resume, networking, applying for a job, or learning a new skill.
- Even if it feels like a small action, trust that it's moving you closer to your goal.
- Action shows the universe that you are ready to receive the career you desire.

Personal Perspective: My Journey with Career Manifestation

For me, focusing on manifesting my ideal career was a transformative process. For years, I struggled with doubts and limiting beliefs about what I was capable of professionally. But once I became clear about my desires and took the time to visualize my dream career, things started to shift.

I also had to confront my own fears. I realized I was afraid of success and worried that I wouldn't be able to handle the responsibilities of my dream job. But once I acknowledged those fears and replaced them with empowering beliefs, I felt confident in my ability to attract the right opportunities.

Taking small, consistent steps was key. I remember updating my LinkedIn profile and reaching out to potential mentors, even though I was nervous. Those actions, combined with my focused energy, helped me attract a job that aligned with my passions and values.

Sealing the Practice: Aligning Your Energy with Career

Aspirations
Today is all about aligning your energy with your career goals and taking inspired action to bring your dream work life into reality. Whether you're looking for a new job, promotion, or even considering a career change, clarity, belief in yourself, and taking the necessary steps are key to success.

As you move forward, remember that manifestation in your career is not just about waiting for things to happen—it's about putting yourself in alignment with the work you desire and taking actionable steps every day. Keep your vision clear, trust in your abilities, and take the necessary steps to make your career goals a reality.

Tomorrow, we'll be focusing on manifesting wealth and abundance, so get ready to expand your financial possibilities. Keep moving forward, and trust that your dream career is within your reach!

"I love my career as it allows me to grow and makes me financially abundant."

Day 19

Creating a wholesome life-
Focus on Wealth & Lifestyle

Welcome to Day 19! Today, we're focusing on manifesting wealth and abundance in your life. Whether you are seeking financial freedom, growing your savings, or simply desiring a lifestyle that aligns with your dreams, today's exercises will help you shift your energy toward attracting wealth and abundance.

Why Focus on Wealth & Lifestyle?

Manifesting wealth is not just about attracting money; it's about creating a lifestyle that reflects the abundance you deserve. Wealth is a tool that supports your freedom, growth, and happiness. Your mindset around wealth and lifestyle shapes your reality and plays a key role in how you experience financial abundance.
When you align with the energy of abundance, wealth flows to you more easily. You create space for greater opportunities and experiences that support your ideal lifestyle.

Exercise: Manifest Wealth and a Fulfilling Lifestyle

1. Define Your Vision of Wealth

Before you can manifest wealth, it's important to have a clear idea of what wealth means to you. Wealth can take many forms, from financial freedom to fulfilling relationships or even personal growth.

- What does wealth look like to you?
- What do you want to do with your wealth?
- How will your life change when you have the abundance you desire?
- Think beyond just money and consider how wealth can enhance your lifestyle.
- Examples:
    - "I am financially abundant and able to travel freely around the world."
    - "I live a luxurious, yet peaceful life filled with meaningful experiences."
    - "I have the financial freedom to support my loved ones and live my dream lifestyle."

2. Cultivate a Prosperity Mindset

Wealth and abundance are not just about accumulating money—they're about your mindset. Today, shift your thoughts to match the energy of abundance.

- Recognize any limiting beliefs you may have about money or wealth.
    - Example: "Money is hard to come by" or "I'll never be wealthy."
- Replace those beliefs with empowering ones.
    - Example: "Wealth is abundant and flows to me easily" or "I am worthy of living a luxurious life."
- Practice daily affirmations of abundance.
    - Example: "I attract unlimited wealth and opportunities into my life every day."
- "I am a magnet for abundance in all areas of my life."

3. Visualize Your Wealth and Ideal Lifestyle

Visualization is one of the most powerful manifestation tools. When you focus on the feelings and experiences of your desired lifestyle, you align yourself with the energy of wealth.

- Close your eyes and picture your ideal life.
- Imagine living in your dream home, experiencing financial freedom, and enjoying the lifestyle that supports your happiness and goals.
- See yourself shopping for things you love, traveling to exotic destinations, and living in luxury, if that aligns with your desires.
- Engage all your senses—what does it feel like? What does your ideal environment smell like, look like, sound like?
- Feel the emotions associated with wealth, such as gratitude, joy, and excitement.

4. Take Inspired Action Toward Your Wealth Goals

Manifestation is not just about sitting back and waiting for things to happen. It's about actively engaging with the universe and taking steps toward your goals.

- Identify small, inspired actions you can take today to move closer to your financial goals.
- Example: Look into new investment opportunities, start a savings plan, or research ways to increase your income.
- Even if it's just an idea, write it down and follow through with it.
- Take practical steps that support your financial abundance and reflect your belief that wealth is on its way to you.

5. Practice Gratitude for Your Current Abundance

Gratitude is one of the most powerful tools for attracting more abundance. When you focus on what you already have, you signal to the universe that you are open to receiving more.

- Take a moment to reflect on all the abundance you

currently have in your life.
- List five things you are grateful for—this could include your health, the people around you, or even small things like your favorite cup of coffee.
- Practice the feeling of gratitude in your body, and imagine your gratitude growing as you continue to attract more wealth and opportunities.

Personal Perspective: My Journey with Wealth Manifestation

When I first started manifesting wealth, I realized I had a lot of limiting beliefs around money. Growing up, I was told that money was scarce and that I had to work extremely hard to earn a living. These beliefs kept me stuck in a cycle of fear and lack.

But once I started focusing on abundance and shifting my mindset, everything changed. I began visualizing my dream lifestyle—traveling, owning a beautiful home, and enjoying financial freedom. I started to see opportunities for wealth where I hadn't before, like new business ventures and investment opportunities.

I also learned the power of gratitude. Each time I was grateful for the money I had, I found that more came to me, and it felt like I was always in the right place at the right time. The more I practiced this mindset and took inspired action, the more wealth I attracted, both in financial abundance and in fulfilling experiences.

Sealing the Practice: Cultivating Wealth Consciousness

Today, you are taking a major step toward manifesting wealth and the lifestyle of your dreams. Remember that wealth is not just about money—it's about the experiences, freedom, and opportunities that come with abundance. By shifting your mindset, visualizing your desired lifestyle, and taking inspired action, you create the foundation for wealth to flow into your life.

"I am grateful for the abundance that I have and the abundance on its way."

Day 20

Maintaining Your Frequency

•••
••

Maintaining a high vibrational frequency throughout the day is essential for effective manifestation. Emotions, as expressions of energy, influence our reality; positive emotions like joy and love elevate our frequency, while negative emotions can lower it. By regularly monitoring and consciously shifting our emotional state, we align ourselves with experiences that reflect our desires, leading to a life of peace, joy, and abundance. Importantly, we possess the ability to transform these energies internally, independent of external circumstances.

In essence, by embracing the practice of emotional monitoring and consciously elevating our vibrational frequency, we become active participants in shaping our reality, inviting experiences that reflect our highest aspirations.

Exercise 1: Frequency Checker - Track Your Emotional State

Purpose: To become aware of your emotional frequency and track where you are throughout the day.

Instructions:

1. **Create Two Lists:**
    - **Positive Emotions**: Write down the emotions you associate with a high frequency (joy, love, peace, gratitude, etc.).

- **Negative Emotions**: Write down emotions tied to a lower frequency (fear, anger, sadness, anxiety, etc.).

2. **2. Scan Your Day:** Throughout the day, check in with yourself and see which emotions you are experiencing. If you find that positive emotions dominate, that means you're attracting a high-frequency reality. If negative emotions are more frequent, you're attracting experiences that mirror those emotions.

3. **3. Reflection:** After going through your emotional check, take note of where you stand. Are you more aligned with positive or negative emotions? Use this information to help raise your frequency moving forward.

Exercise 2: Water Technique - Shift Your Energy

Purpose: To clear negative emotions and raise your frequency using the power of water.

Instructions:

1. **Set an Alarm:** Set an hourly reminder on your phone or clock to prompt you to check in on your emotional state.
2. **If Positive Emotions:**
    - If you're feeling positive emotions, take a moment to congratulate yourself for maintaining a high frequency. Drink a glass of water, allowing it to recharge your energy as you stay in that positive state. Water, as proven by Dr. Emoto's research, holds energy, and by drinking it while feeling positive emotions, you are helping to raise your own frequency.
3. **If Negative Emotions:**

- Hold a glass of water and reflect on your current negative emotions. Feel them deeply, but understand they are only energy. Imagine that these emotions are transferring into the water. Once you feel this transfer, dispose of the water, symbolizing the release of negative energy.
- For more intense emotions like anger, stress, or anxiety, hold the water near your third eye center (forehead). Imagine these negative energies pouring into the glass. Then, dispose of the water, as a symbolic release of those emotions.

4. **Shift Your Frequency:**
   - After releasing negative emotions, create a new list of opposite positive emotions. For example, if you were feeling "Anger," write "Calm."
   - Hold a fresh glass of water to your third eye, and while focusing on the new positive emotions, affirm to yourself:
     - "I am feeling calm and relaxed."
     - "I am peaceful and at ease."
     - "All is well in my world."
     - Drink the water, allowing it to fully charge your frequency with the new positive emotions.

Exercise 3: Whiteboard Technique - Clear Your Emotions Mentally

Purpose: To mentally erase negative emotions and replace them with high-frequency feelings.

Instructions:

1. **Set an Alarm:** As with the Water Technique, set an hourly reminder to check in on your emotional state.

2. Visualization:
   - Imagine a whiteboard in front of you. On this

whiteboard, see yourself writing down all the low-frequency emotions you're experiencing. These are the emotions you wish to clear.

3. **Erasure Process:**
   - Using a violet-colored eraser in your mind's eye, start erasing these negative emotions one by one. Visualize the words disappearing completely.

4. **Rewriting with Positivity:**
   - Once the negative emotions are erased, visualize yourself writing new, positive emotions on the board. Imagine how these emotions feel. Hold the image and experience the emotions in your body.

5. **Gratitude**:
   - Conclude the exercise by thanking the universe for helping you shift your energy. Acknowledge the power you have to change your frequency.

Remember, you have the power to change your emotional state at any moment. Simply become aware, shift your frequency, and align with your highest self. This practice is your key to manifesting the life you truly desire.

These exercises, when practiced consistently, will not only help you become aware of your current emotional state but also empower you to change it at any moment, raising your frequency and aligning you with your highest desires. Keep practicing, and you will see the transformation unfold, one step at a time.

"I consciously choose thoughts that elevate my energy."

Day 21

Daily Manifestation Routine

⁙

Now that you've worked through days of powerful manifestation practices, you've built a strong foundation. To continue your manifestation journey, it's essential to establish a daily routine that aligns with the practices you've explored. This routine will help keep you centered, focused, and in alignment with your desires.

Here's a comprehensive daily manifestation routine based on the exercises from the past 20 days. Feel free to adjust the timing and details to suit your needs. The key is consistency and intentionality.

Morning Routine (Start your day with intention)

1. Wake Up with Gratitude (5 minutes)

- As soon as you wake up, express gratitude for the new day. This sets a positive tone and helps you attract more of what you're thankful for.
- Say aloud or write in your journal:
    - "I am grateful for this new day and all the opportunities it holds."
    - "I am grateful for everything I already have, and I am open to receiving more."

2. Invoke for divine guidance

No matter what form of divinity you believe in, take a

moment each day to acknowledge and connect with this higher power. Just as we were taught to greet our parents upon waking as children, begin your day by greeting the Divine with reverence and gratitude

- Imagine divine light pouring down from above, be surrounded by it.
- As it dawns upon you, mentally bow down to this light and greet it.
- Give thanks for its powerful blessings.
- Imagine this divine light encircling you in a ring of protection and guidance.

Affirmations (5 minutes)

- Recite your daily affirmations to align your energy with your desires.
- Read your list of important goals/desires from each area
- Energize one important goal of yours.
- Repeat them aloud or silently as many times as you feel compelled to. Allow the words to sink in and shift your mindset.

3. Meditation for Clarity (10 minutes)

- Sit in your sacred space or a quiet spot. Close your eyes and take deep, calming breaths.
- Visualize a white light entering your body and clearing away any doubts or negativity.
- Focus on your breath for 5-10 minutes to center yourself.
- Reflect on what you want to accomplish today, in the present tense as if they have already been accomplished.
- Immerse yourself in the experience, seeing yourself living your desires.
- Use all five senses—see the colors, hear the sounds, and feel the textures. Get as detailed as possible.

- Close with gratitude.

4. Small Inspired Action

- Take at least one small, inspired action toward your goals. Manifestation requires you to show up and take action.
- It could be sending an email, making a call, researching something you're passionate about, or taking a moment to enjoy a small win.
- The action should feel aligned with your desires and create momentum.

5. Check Your Frequency (2 hourly)

- Reflect on any limiting beliefs that may arise during the day. When you catch negative thoughts, pause and reframe them. To mentally erase negative emotions and replace them with high-frequency feelings, use the techniques shared on day 20. Choose the one that speaks to you.

Close the day with clarity and gratitude

6. Reflection and Journaling (10-15 minutes)

- Reflect on your day and how you felt throughout it.
    - What went well?
    - What challenges did you encounter?
    - How did you take inspired action today?
- Write about your experiences and any breakthroughs you had.
    - Example: "Today I focused on my health and felt so energized after my workout!"
    - "I took a small step towards my career goal by reaching out to someone for advice."

7. Gratitude Practice (5 minutes)

- End your day by writing down at least 3 things you are grateful for. This helps you close the day on a positive note and keeps you in an abundant mindset.
  - "I am grateful for the supportive people in my life."
  - "I am grateful for the progress I made today."
  - "I am grateful for the abundance that flows into my life every day."

8. Affirmations for the Night (5 minutes)

- Before going to sleep, repeat your affirmations again.
- Visualize yourself already living your desires, experiencing the emotions associated with them.
- As you drift off to sleep, feel gratitude for everything you're manifesting, knowing it is already on its way.

Weekly Add-ons (Optional but recommended)

1. Vision Board Update (Every Week)(Refer to Day 8)

- Dedicate some time once a week to update or review your vision board.
- Add new images that reflect any new desires or goals.
- Feel into the excitement and energy of seeing your vision come to life.

2. Fire Ritual (Every Week or as Needed)

- Use a fire ritual (or any other clearing ritual) to release any lingering negative energy or resistance.
- Write down anything you're ready to let go of, burn the paper, and release those limiting beliefs or fears into the fire.

Personal Perspective: My Daily Manifestation Journey

When I first started incorporating a daily manifestation routine, I was skeptical about how much of a difference it could make. But what I found was that consistency is key. By dedicating even just a few minutes each morning to set my intentions and visualize my goals, I began to notice subtle shifts in my life.

Each time I took inspired action, even if small, I felt more aligned with my desires. And over time, this practice helped me manifest bigger dreams into my reality.

The most impactful part of my routine has been the gratitude practice. It truly helped me shift my mindset from lack to abundance. Now, I wake up excited for the day, knowing that everything I want is already on its way. And when challenges arise, I now feel empowered to reframe any limiting beliefs, trusting in my ability to overcome them.

Your dreams are waiting for you—let's make them a reality, one day at a time.

"I am the creator of my reality, and I manifest my desires effortlessly."

Embracing Your Manifestation Journey

Congratulations on completing 21 Days of Manifestation! You have embarked on a powerful journey of transformation, aligning your energy, thoughts, and actions with the life you truly desire. Over these 21 days, you have tapped into your innate ability to create, evolve, and manifest your deepest aspirations.

Manifestation is not merely a process; it is a way of being. It is about continuously aligning your intentions with your higher self, trusting in the universe, and allowing divine energy to guide your path. This journey has provided you with tools and practices that are not just for these 21 days, but for a lifetime of conscious creation.

Spiritualizing Your Goals: Aligning with Divine Energy

It is easy to focus solely on the practical aspects of manifestation—setting goals, taking action, and maintaining a positive mindset. However, true manifestation is about more than just tangible outcomes; it is about spiritual alignment. When you spiritualize your goals, you surrender the need for control and place your trust in the divine flow of the universe. Whether you call it the universe, source energy, or divine guidance, there is a greater force working in your favor. By embracing faith and trust, you allow your desires to manifest with greater ease and purpose.

Spiritualizing your goals does not mean passively waiting for results—it means co-creating with the universe. It means setting clear intentions, following inner guidance, and taking inspired action while remaining open to divine timing. The more you align with this energy, the more effortlessly your manifestations unfold.

Moving Forward with Faith and Trust

This journey doesn't end here. Manifestation is a lifelong practice, one that evolves as you grow. To continue harnessing the power of manifestation, it's essential to stay connected to your intentions by regularly revisiting your goals to ensure they align with your highest self. Trust in divine timing by releasing the need for control and believing that everything is unfolding as it should. Align yourself with abundance by cultivating gratitude, generosity, and positive energy to maintain a high vibrational state. Follow your inner guidance, trusting that the universe communicates through intuition, synchronicities, and inner wisdom. Embrace the journey, recognizing that growth, expansion, and discovery are integral parts of the process, and enjoy each step along the way.

Your Manifestations Are Already Unfolding

By integrating these principles into your daily life, you have stepped into a space of limitless possibility. Your dreams are not distant—they are already in motion. The universe is always conspiring in your favor, guiding you toward your highest potential. Trust in your journey, release doubt, and embrace the infinite opportunities that await you.

You are a powerful creator. Your dreams are valid. Your desires are destined to unfold. Keep believing, keep shining, and keep manifesting.

The universe is waiting for you to claim your greatness.

With love power and abundant blessings

About The Authors: Thought Partners

Nutan Khurana

Nutan Khurana is a multifaceted professional whose global exposure enriches her passion for fashion, wellness, and holistic living. As a fashion and wellness consultant, she seamlessly integrates her international experiences with a profound understanding of holistic health, guiding individuals toward achieving their best selves both inside and out.

Beyond her consultancy, Nutan is a certified energy healer, employing diverse modalities to restore balance and vitality to those she serves. Her holistic approach honors the intricate connection between mind, body, and spirit, promoting overall well-being and harmony.

In her role as a manifestation and life coach, Nutan empowers individuals to tap into their inner potential and manifest the lives they desire. Through personalized coaching sessions, she assists individuals in identifying their goals, overcoming limiting beliefs, and harnessing the power of manifestation to turn their dreams into reality.

Manisha Abbasi

Manisha Abbasi's journey is a heartfelt tapestry woven with a deep-seated passion for reigniting the 'Joy of Wholesome Living.' Her collaborations with transformative communities are dedicated to fostering individuals through a comprehensive blend of cognitive, social, and emotional skills, with mindfulness as the cornerstone.

With over 15 years of unwavering commitment to cultivating positive learning environments in the education sector, Manisha's approach is enriched by a diverse array of experiences. Her profound understanding of mindfulness is deeply influenced by the invaluable teachings of Plum Village monks, where each mindful step is seen as a path to recovery, joy, healing, and transformation.

In her role as a master trainer with UNESCO, Manisha not only shapes minds but also nurtures hearts, guiding individuals to align their thoughts and actions with core values through ethical mindfulness. Central to her work is a profound alignment with healing modalities, which has deepened her understanding of how our thoughts and beliefs profoundly influence our lives. Through her soulful workshops, she empowers individuals to embrace self-love and harness their innate abilities, guiding them to craft the lives they truly desire.

Other Published work:

ReCreate Your Destiny

Workshops We Conduct as Part of Our Practice:

- Chakra Journey
- Mindful Weekends
- Manifestation Weekend Retreat
- Empowerment through manifestation
- Inclusive Intentions: Manifestation and Yoga for All

We would love to hear from you:

Email:
essence2expression@gmail.com

Instagram:
@essence2expression2024

Youtube:
https://www.youtube.com/@recreateyourdestiny

Website-
www.essence2expression.co.in